Instant Bible Lessons

Bible Truths

by Pamela J. Kuhn

For information regarding the CPSIA on this printed material call:
203-595-3636 and provide reference # LANC-488550

rainbowpublishers®

Rainbow Publishers • P.O. Box 261129 • San Diego, CA 92196
www.RainbowPublishers.com

Dedicated to . . .

My parents, Carl and Dorothy Cessna;
my mother-in-law, Helen Kuhn;
and in memory of my father-in-law, Rev. R.L. Kuhn.
You lived by God's Word joyfully and consistently,
inspiring us to build our lives on its firm foundation.

INSTANT BIBLE LESSONS: BIBLE TRUTHS
© 2013 by Rainbow Publishers, eighteenth printing
ISBN 10: 1-885358-28-8
ISBN 13: 978-1-885358-28-8
Rainbow reorder# RB36622
RELIGION / Christian Ministry / Children

Rainbow Publishers
P.O. Box 261129
San Diego, CA 92196
www.RainbowPublishers.com

Cover Illustrator: Phyllis Harris
Interior Illustrators: Joel Ryan, Roger Johnson

Scriptures are from the *Holy Bible: New International Version* (North American Edition), copyright ©1973, 1978, 1984 by the International Bible Society. Used by permission of Zondervan Bible Publishers.

Printed in the United States of America

Contents

Introduction 5
How to Use This Book 5

Chapter 1: God Gave Me My Bible 7
Memory Verse Scroll 8
WBBL 9
Used by God 10
Fading and Enduring 11
Withering Grass and Falling Flowers 12
The Singing Band 13
Flower Piñata 14
The Bible Is... 15

Chapter 2: My Bible Teaches Me Respect 17
Letter to Pastor 18
Bears and Bells 19
Respectful Rhyming 20
Caged Bears 21
Dot-to-Dot Surprises 22
Rebus Story 23
Jiggly Bears 24
We Love You, Pastor! 25

Chapter 3: My Bible Teaches Me Responsibility ..27
Crown Confusion 28
I Want to Do What's Right 29
That's What the Bible Says 30
Responsible Like Joash 31
I Am Responsible When 32
Responsibility Mobile 33
God's House 34
Child Kings 35

Chapter 4: My Bible Teaches Me Kindness 37
Love Chain 38
Help Me Get to the King 39
Can I Be Kind? 40
Hand-Clapping Kindness 41
Keeping Promises 42
Partner Fun 43
Mephibosheth 44
Kindness to All God's Creatures 45

Chapter 5: My Bible Teaches Me Generosity 47
Fishy Word Search 48
Sharing Multiplies Happiness 49

Verse Purse 50
When I Go to Church 51
Time to Share 52
Sharing 53
Generous With Me 54
Bread and Fish 55

Chapter 6: My Bible Teaches Me Obedience 57
Fish Swimmer 58
Where is Jonah? 59
Coming Clean 60
Yummy Boats of Obedience 61
A Tale from a Fish 62
Jonah in Sequence 63
Nutty Obedience 65

Chapter 7: My Bible Teaches Me Forgiveness 67
Forgiveness Game 68
David's Forgiveness Knife 69
Telling the Story 70
Scrambled Mess 71
Forgiving Makes Me Happy 72
David's Spear 73
Army Puppets 74

Chapter 8: My Bible Teaches Me Honesty 77
Memory Verse Mail 78
Honesty Pantomime 79
True or False 80
Helpful Story Tellers 81
Singin' About the Bible 83
Too Many Lies? 84
My Bag of Coins Reminder 85

Chapter 9: Miscellaneous Bible Activities 87
Dear Parent 87
Supply Help 88
Bible Tree 89
Bible Charades 90
"My Bible Teaches Me" Review 91
Secret Message 92
Wiggle Busters for Little Bible Readers 93
Bible Bookmarks 94
Commemorative Stamps 95

Answers to Puzzles 96

Introduction

What does the <u>Bible</u> teach us? Is it "just another book" that gives us ideas for how to live better? No! <u>It is God's own Word, an enduring Word that will never pass away.</u> The principles taught in the Bible are not optional.

In *Bible Truths,* your students will learn what the Bible teaches. Through creative role-playing, games, songs, stories and much more, you can plant the seed that will grow into the love of God's Word in the hearts of your students.

Each of the first eight chapters includes a Bible story, memory verse and numerous activities to help reinforce the truth in the lesson. An additional chapter contains miscellaneous projects that can be used anytime throughout the study. Teacher aids are also sprinkled throughout the book, including bulletin board ideas and discussion starters.

As you work through the lessons, you may use your own judgment as to the appropriateness of the projects for your class. Everything in this book is designed to meet the 5 to 10 age range, however some activities may be more appealing to a younger group while others will more readily meet the abilities of older children.

The most exciting aspect of the *Instant Bible Lessons* series, which includes *God's Angels, Virtues and Values* and *Talking to God* as well as *Bible Truths,* is its flexibility. You can easily adapt these lessons to a Sunday School hour, a children's church service, a Wednesday night Bible study or home use. And, because there is a variety of reproducible ideas from which to choose (see below), you will enjoy creating a class session that is best for your group of students—whether large or small, beginning or advanced, active or studious. Plus, the intriguing topics will keep your kids coming back for more, week after week.

Let's teach God's Word, making our students "wise for salvation." After all, isn't our ultimate goal to equip our students with the knowledge of the Bible so they may find salvation, daily help and guidance through its pages? Bless you as you embark on this important endeavor.

How to Use This Book

Each chapter begins with a Bible story which you may read to your class, followed by discussion questions. Then, use any or all of the activities in the chapter to help drive home the message of that lesson. All of the activities are tagged with one of the icons below, so you can quickly flip through the chapter and select the projects you need. Simply cut off the teacher instructions on the pages and duplicate as desired. Also, see pages 87 and 88 for reproducible notes you can fill in and send home to parents.

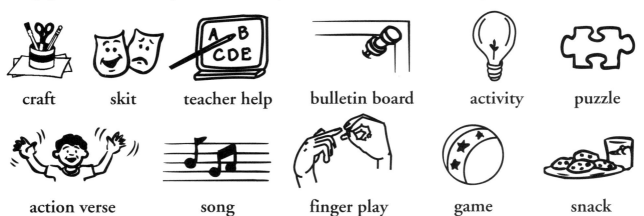

craft   skit   teacher help   bulletin board   activity   puzzle

action verse   song   finger play   game   snack

Chapter 1
God Gave Me My Bible

Memory Verse

The grass withers and the flowers fall, but the word of the Lord stands forever. 1 Peter 1:24-25

Brainstorm what is the Bible?

Story to Share
The Enduring Word

The priests and prophets of Judah wanted Jeremiah dead! Why? Jeremiah had prophesied against the city of Judah. He had said: "The Lord sent me to prophecy against this city. Stop the sinful things you are doing and obey the voice of God. If you don't, God will make this city a curse to all the nations of the earth."

The name of God was still important to the elders and the people of the land, so even though the priests and prophets wanted to kill Jeremiah, they couldn't do it. But the king did ban him from the temple.

While Jeremiah was banned, God sent him a message and told him to write it down. Jeremiah could not write fast or neatly so he called for Baruch, a scribe who was used to writing, to record the words God was telling him. Baruch wrote what Jeremiah dictated in a book made of rolled parchment paper. Day after day for several months Baruch wrote the words Jeremiah heard from the Lord.

Then Jeremiah said, "Baruch, I am not permitted to go to the temple. You take these words and read them in the temple. Maybe people will hear these words and turn from their evil ways."

Baruch did exactly what Jeremiah asked him. One group of people heard it and told another group. Eventually the princes heard it and were frightened by it. They decided that the king should hear it.

Jehudi, one of the king's pages, fetched the scroll and read it to the king. The king heard only a few words when he flew into a rage. "Give me that scroll," said the king. "I'll show you what I think of the words written on it." He drew out a knife, grabbed the scroll, cut it and threw it into the fire, letting it burn until it was destroyed.

"Where are Jeremiah and Baruch?" the king asked. "Bring them to me." Then he signed a warrant for their arrest.

But Jeremiah and Baruch were hidden away, where Baruch again wrote the words that God gave to Jeremiah. This second edition contained much of what is in the Bible's book of Jeremiah today. It also contained the prophecy of what would happen to King Jehoiakim. All of the prophecy came true. Jehoiakim finished his days in defeat because he would not listen to and obey the laws and words of God. God's words cannot be destroyed!

— based on Jeremiah 36:1-32

Questions for Discussion

1. Can you think of a verse from the Bible which you can say from memory?
2. Can anyone ever make you forget that verse against your will?

craft

Memory Verse Scroll

Materials
• scroll, duplicated
• drinking straws
• glue
• scissors

Directions
1. Have the students cut out the scroll.
2. Show how to glue the ends to two straws and roll it toward the middle.
3. Have the children pretend that they are the scribe, Baruch, writing God's words on the scroll.

God Gave Me My Bible

The grass withers and the flowers fall, but the word of the Lord stands forever. 1 Peter 1:24-25

WBBL

Characters: Timmy Tell, Anchor Person
Billy Bell, Reporter

TT: Good morning, boys and girls. This is Timmy Tell with WBBL and *The News Today.* Our top story today comes from the palace. The prophet Jeremiah claims to have words from God and Jehudi is going to read them to the king. Our reporter, Billy Bell, is standing by. Billy, what's happening there in the temple?

BB: Timmy, things are really in an uproar right now here in the palace. Jehudi has just read the scroll to the king. It's an account of fatal consequences if the nation does not turn from their sin. The king is very angry. Oh, my, oh, my.

TT: Billy, Billy, are you there? It seems like we have temporarily lost our reporter. He was saying that the king is very angry over the words Jeremiah has written and has said to be from God. Billy, are you there?

BB: Yes, Timmy, I am now outside the palace. I was afraid for my life inside. The king was so angry that he cut Jeremiah's scroll with his knife and then threw the scroll in the fire. He has also made a warrant for Jeremiah's arrest. It doesn't look good for the prophet.

TT: What do you think, Billy? You heard the words. Do you think they were from God?

BB: Yes, Timmy, I do. My heart was stirred when I heard them read. I think that is what made the king so angry. He knew it, too, but he didn't want to admit to it.

TT: Thank you Billy, for that live coverage from the palace. This is WBBL, Timmy Tell reporting.

Usage

Children enjoy playing "pretend." Select two students for the roles of Timmy and Billy. Encourage them to act out the parts with emphasis. Afterward, relate the skit to present day and ask the class to imagine what it would be like if someone would go to our U.S. President with news like Jeremiah's. Have them tell what they think would happen.

God Gave Me My Bible

Used by God

craft

• • • • • • • • • • •

Materials

- boy and girl, duplicated
- crayons
- scissors
- drinking straws or craft sticks
- tape

Directions

1. Have the students color and cut out the boy and girl.
2. Show how to tape a straw or stick to the back of each figure.
3. Allow the children to use their puppets to tell each other: "God's Word Endures" and to quote a Bible verse.

Discuss

Say, **Baruch was willing to be used.** He wrote down every word that God gave to Jeremiah. <u>What are some ways you can help others hear what God says to us in His Word?</u>

Fading and Enduring

puzzle

In the puzzle below, look for the names of things that wither and fall. Words are spelled across, up, down, and backward. Some letters are used more than once. How many can you find?

Words to Find:
- rose
- pansy
- iris
- peony
- grass
- tulip
- mum
- daisy
- violet

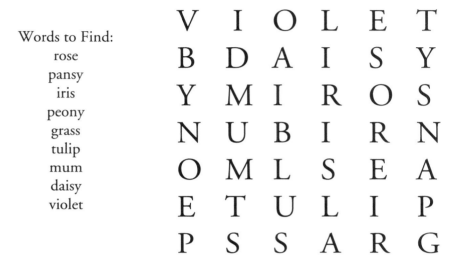

```
V  I  O  L  E  T
B  D  A  I  S  Y
Y  M  I  R  O  S
N  U  B  I  R  N
O  M  L  S  E  A
E  T  U  L  I  P
P  S  S  A  R  G
```

Materials
• puzzle, duplicated
• pencils

Usage

Explain to the class what "wither" means. All of the words in the puzzle are flowers, except for "grass." The word list is on page 96 — you may want to provide the list for younger children.

Now write the leftover letters on the line below to find out what shall endure forever.

___ ___ ___ ___ ___ ___ ___

Solution is on page 96.

God Gave Me My Bible

craft

Materials
- picture, duplicated
- construction paper, cut 1" larger on all sides than the picture
- crayons
- scissors
- fresh-pulled grass and flowers
- glue

Directions
1. Have the class color and cut out the picture.
2. Show how to glue the picture to the center of the sheet of construction paper.
3. Allow them to glue some grass and flower pieces on the picture.
4. Say, **Look at the grass and flowers tomorrow and see how long they last. They will fade but remember, God's Word lasts forever!**

Withering Grass and Falling Flowers

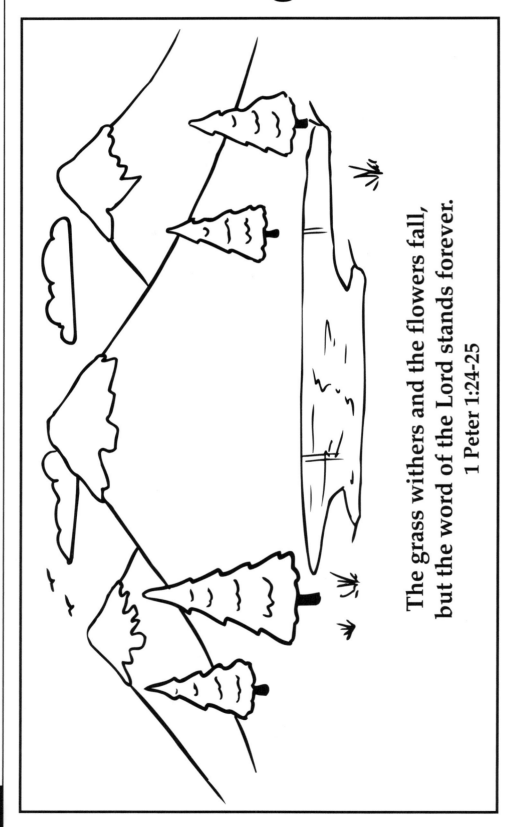

The grass withers and the flowers fall, but the word of the Lord stands forever. 1 Peter 1:24-25

The Singing Band

God's Lasting Word

God's Word will last for all our days,
For all our days, for all our days.
God's Word will last for all our days,
I will clap and sing.
I will clap and sing.
I will clap and sing.
God's Word will last for all our days,
I will clap and sing.

song

• • • • • • • • • •

Materials
•instruments, dupli-
cated
•crayons
•scissors

Directions
1. Have the students color and cut out the instruments.
2. Ask the students to select one instrument. Tell them they are to use their voices to represent the instrument they have.
3. Sing and clap through the song once to the tune of "Fishers of Men."
4. Repeat the song with the "band" playing their instruments as you and any other adults continue to sing the words.
5. Repeat the song several times, allowing the children to change instruments as they wish.

Cymbals

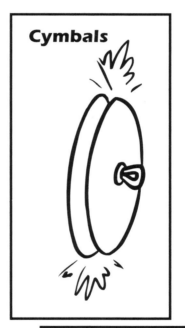

Saxophone

Flute

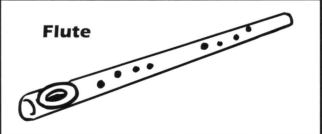

Trumpet

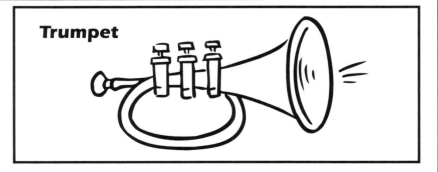

God Gave Me My Bible

13

Flower Piñata

Materials
- flowers, duplicated
- three large grocery bags
- wrapped candy
- wire hanger
- stapler
- markers
- rope
- plastic baseball bat

Directions
1. Place the bags inside each other.
2. Fill with candy.
3. Fold the open ends of the bag over the hanger and staple them.
4. Decorate the outside of the bag by cutting out and coloring the flowers and grass at right, as desired.
5. Hang the piñata from a high place with rope.
6. Blindfold each child and give the students a turn at "destroying" the flowers and grass. As they swing, they should say, "God's Word endures forever."

God Gave Me My Bible

The Bible Is...

What do you think the Bible is?
Here are some ideas.
Write yours on the lines beside them.

B   Believable   _____

I   Incredible   _____

B   Bold   _____

L   Love   _____

E   Enduring   _____

We also call the Bible "God's Word."
Can you do the same thing with the letters from God's Word?

G   _____

O   _____

D   _____

S   _____

W   _____

O   _____

R   _____

D   _____

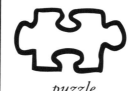

puzzle

• • • • • • • • • •

Materials
•puzzle, duplicated
•pencils

Usage
There are, obviously, no absolute answers to these puzzles. After everyone is finished, have the students read their answers aloud. Comment on each one, relating how the word is applicable to the Bible. Praise the children for their creativity.

Chapter 2

My Bible Teaches Me Respect

Memory Verse

Show proper respect to everyone: Love the brotherhood of believers.
1 Peter 2:17

Story to Share
Disrespectful Youth

The people of Israel had turned against God. King Ahab married Jezebel and she persuaded him to worship Baal, a false god. Now the people were following the example of their king.

Amid all the wickedness there was a great and brave prophet of God named Elijah. He was hated because he had messages that had been given to him by God and he was faithful to deliver these messages from God. His life was dedicated to bringing Israel back to the true God.

There was a younger man, Elisha, who became good friends with Elijah. One day Elijah said, "Elisha, the time has come for me to go to heaven. What can I do for you?" "Oh, Elijah, treat me as your eldest son and give me a double portion of the Spirit of God within you," answered Elisha.

"Yes, Elisha. This I will do if you see me taken from you," Elijah replied.

While they were talking, a chariot of flames, drawn by horses of fire, came between them. Elijah was swept off the ground with a huge blast of wind and taken to heaven. The spirit of Elijah was now with Elisha.

Later, Elisha was walking along the road to Bethel when he heard a commotion and looked up. There were some young men coming out of the town, pointing at Elisha and laughing. "Go on up, you baldhead!" one yelled. "Why don't you find yourself a chariot and go to heaven, too?" jeered another.

Elisha turned around and saw that they were the same young people who laughed at those who attended the School of the Prophets in Bethel. They called the scholars bad names and tried to drive them from the town.

For several minutes Elisha ignored the youth, but they were insistent. Finally, he must have realized that they were not showing disrespect to him, but to God, whom Elisha loved. Suddenly, he called down punishment from heaven on the boys.

No sooner had the words left his mouth than two bears came out of the woods and killed 42 children. Disrespect to a prophet or preacher of God will never be tolerated!

— based on 2 Kings 2:23-25

Questions for Discussion

1. Who is our pastor?
2. Does God want us to be respectful to our pastor?

Materials
•letter, duplicated
•envelope
•decorative stickers
•markers or crayons

Directions
1. Have the students fill in the pastor's name and their own name at the beginning and end of the letter.
2. On the middle lines, they should tell why they love the pastor.
3. The children may place their completed letters in envelopes that they decorate with stickers, markers or crayons.
4. Encourage the students to give their letters to the pastor with a hug. You may want to share with the pastor prior to this project to expect the letters. Or, invite the pastor to your class for the presentation.

My Bible Teaches Me Respect

Letter to Pastor

Dear Pastor_____,

I respect you because you are God's messenger to me.
I love you because

_____

_____

_____

Thank you for teaching me about God's Word.

Your friend,

_____

Bears and Bells

game

. . . .

Materials
- bears, duplicated to brown paper
- scissors
- yarn
- jingle bells
- clothesline or rope
- clothespins
- bean bag or soft ball

Directions
1. Duplicate and cut out eight bears.
2. Tie yarn with a jingle bell around each bear's neck.
3. Write one answer (at left) on each bear.
4. Hang the bears on the clothesline.
5. Divide into teams. Ask the questions at left, then have a child throw the bean bag at the correct answer. If the bell jingles, the team gets 5 points. If the child aims at the correct answer and doesn't hit it, the team gets 2 points.

Questions and Answers

1. Who was king of Israel at the time of our story? *Ahab*

2. Who was the great prophet of God who dedicated his life to bring Israel back to the true God? *Elijah*

3. Who received a double portion of the Spirit of God when he saw Elijah taken from him to heaven? *Elisha*

4. What did Elijah leave in to go to heaven? *chariot of fire*

5. Where was Elisha walking to ? *Bethel*

6. What were the young men calling Elisha? *"baldhead"*

7. What came out of the woods and killed the young men? *bears*

8. When we show disrespect to a man of God we are showing disrespect to whom? *God*

Reference — 2 Kings 2:23-25

My Bible Teaches Me Respect

puzzle

Materials
•puzzle, duplicated
•pencils

Usage

This puzzle may be completed by your older children individually or with younger kids in a group setting. Even kindergartners can suggest rhyming words with you as you call out, "Blow. Say some words that sound like 'blow.'" For fun, try to fit the words they suggest into the verse to see if they work. After the verse is completed, help the class memorize it.

My Bible Teaches Me Respect

Respectful Rhyming

Find a word that rhymes with the one under the line
to complete the memory verse.

_____   pro_____
      Blow   sir

respect _____   every_____:
            do   sun

_____   _____
     Dove   see

_____hood of _____lievers.
   mother   he

1 _____2:17
        meter

Solution is on page 96.

20

Caged Bears

*Show proper respect to everyone:
Love the brotherhood of believers.*
1 Peter 2:17

craft

. . . .

Materials
- bears and verse, duplicated
- markers
- white paper
- construction paper
- scissors
- glue
- rulers

Directions
1. Have the class color and cut out the bears and verse.
2. Instruct them to measure and cut five ½" x 11" strips from white paper.
3. They should glue the bears and verse to a vertical piece of construction paper.
4. Have them glue the strips on the bears to "cage" them.
5. On the strips, they should write the names or titles of people whom they can respect.

My Bible Teaches Me Respect

21

Dot-to-Dot Surprises

puzzle/game

• • • • • • • • • •

Materials
- puzzle and stand, duplicated to heavy paper
- crayons
- wide tip marker
- scissors

Directions

1. Have the students say the memory verse as they connect the dots with the marker, then allow them to color the picture.

2. Instruct them to cut out the bear on the lines they made, and to cut out the stand.

3. They should snip the stand at the two solid lines, then fold at the dashed line. The stand will hold the bear's legs.

4. Say, **Let's get rid of disrespect. Pick a partner and have a race blowing your bears across the table. Make them fall down so they can't run after us!**

My Bible Teaches Me Respect

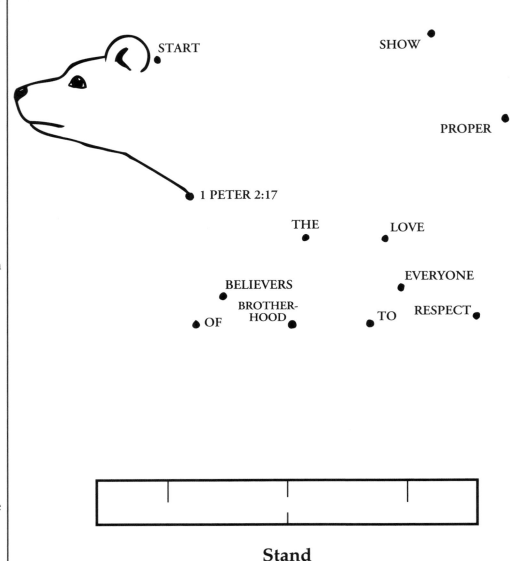

START

SHOW

PROPER

1 PETER 2:17

THE

LOVE

BELIEVERS

EVERYONE

BROTHER-HOOD

OF

TO   RESPECT

Stand

Rebus Story

puzzle

I am a happy _____.

I love to go to _____.

I like to sing songs, _____.

and listen to the _____.

tell me about _____.

Solution is on page 96.

I WILL
Show proper respect to everyone:
Love the brotherhood of believers.
1 Peter 2:17

Materials
- puzzle, pictures and label, duplicated
- crayons or markers
- scissors
- glue
- envelopes

Directions
1. Have the students color and cut out the puzzle, pictures and label.
2. They should glue the label to the front of an envelope.
3. Show how to put the pictures in place as you read the "story."
4. Encourage the students to keep their stories in the envelope to review the lesson.

My Bible Teaches Me Respect

Jiggly Bears

snack

• • • • • • • • • •

Materials

- four envelopes of Knox™ gelatin
- three 4 oz. packages of flavored gelatin
- four cups of boiling water
- one 9" x 13" pan and one 8" x 8" pan
- bear cookie cutter, or use pattern at left and a plastic knife

Directions

1. Mix both types of gelatin together.
2. Add boiling water. Stir until dissolved.
3. Pour into two pans (one 9" x 13" and one 8" x 8"). Chill until firm.
4. Allow the children to cut out their own bears, reminding them if they show respect to those around them they may eat the bears instead of the bears eating them!

Optional

Bears may be "decorated" with a can of whipped cream. Have napkins handy!

Recipe for Jiggly Bears

- Four envelopes of Knox™ gelatin
- Three 4 oz. packages of flavored gelatin
- 4 cups of boiling water

Mix the gelatin together and add boiling water (you may want to reduce this recipe to make fewer bears). Stir until dissolved. Chill, then cut into bears using pattern. Remember the story about Elisha and respect others so you may eat the bears instead of the bears eating you!

Show proper respect to everyone: Love the brotherhood of believers.
1 Peter 2:17

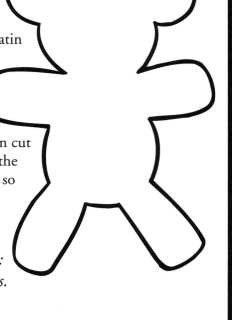

We Love You, Pastor!

bulletin board

. . . .

Materials
- church, duplicated
- large photo of pastor
- scissors
- crayons
- photo of each student and teacher
- lettering: We Love You, Pastor *name*

Directions
1. Post the lettering at the top of the bulletin board.
2. Place the pastor's photo in the center of the board.
3. Have the children cut out and color a church, then write why they love the pastor on it.
4. Place the child's photo and church in a circle around the pastor's photo.

Optional
Invite the pastor to your class and take a picture of him surrounded by the class. Have copies made for each student. Invite the pastor back for an autograph signing!

My Bible Teaches Me Respect

I love our pastor because…

_____

_____

Responsibity:- do what I Know
I have to do.
- At school: to learn, to
do the homework
- At home: to do our chairs,
to help with young siblings
- At church, to clean/respect the
sanctuary.

Chapter 3
My Bible Teaches Me Responsibility

Memory Verse
Guard what has been entrusted to your care. 1 Timothy 6:20

Story to Share
A Responsible King

Eight-year-old Josiah had become king of Judah. Josiah loved God and served Him faithfully.

After he had been king 18 years, Josiah called for his secretary. "I want the temple in Jerusalem to be repaired," he told her. "It has grown shabby and needs to be put in order. Get carpenters, masons and builders and have them restore it."

The repairing began. Every corner of the temple was cleaned. The high priest discovered, hidden in one of the corners, the scroll of God's Law. This scroll was the only copy of the Law the Israelites had.

Josiah listened as the royal scribe, Shaphan, read from the scroll. With an aching heart, Josiah realized that every Law that was written on the scroll had been broken. And these Laws were from God!

"These commandments that I give you today are to be on your hearts," read the scribe. "Impress them on your children. Talk about them when you sit at home, when you walk along the road, when you lie down at night and when you get up."

"If you fully obey the Lord your God and carefully follow all His commandments I give you today, the Lord your God will set you high above the nations on earth. However, if you do not obey the Lord your God and do not carefully obey all His commandments, the Lord will send on you curses, confusion and rebuke in everything you put your hand to, until you are destroyed and come to sudden ruin."

Josiah tore at his clothes, weeping in despair. "We have not been teaching God's Laws. How selfish and contemptible we have become. The Lord must surely be angry with us."

After hearing the message, Josiah called his people together in the temple and read to them the law of God. He took an oath, renewing his covenant in the presence of the Lord. "I will follow the Lord and keep His commands, regulations and decrees with all my heart and soul." The people promised that they, too, would obey God's Laws.

All of Jerusalem rejoiced and God was pleased with Josiah, the responsible King.

— 2 Kings 22:1-13; 23:1-3

Questions for Discussion

1. Is responsibility just for kings or presidents — those "important" people?
2. What things has God entrusted to your care? Are you responsible?

Crown Confusion

Uh-oh. The king got his crowns mixed up
and now the verse doesn't make sense.
Can you help him put them back in order?

Materials
•puzzle, duplicated
•scissors
•glue
•paper or construc-
tion paper

Directions
Have the students cut
out the crowns and
glue them in order on
another sheet of paper
or construction paper.

Solution is on page 96.

28

I Want to Do What's Right

Song

name wants to do what's right.

name wants to do what's right.

Yip, yeah, dee dippy do dee,

Responsible he will be.

2 Kings 22-23

Materials

- crown and robe, duplicated
- plastic spoons
- markers
- glue
- scissors

Directions

1. Have the students color and cut out the crown and robe.
2. Instruct the class to draw eyes, mouth and cheeks on the back of the spoon.
3. Allow them to glue the crown and robe to the spoon.
4. Ask everyone to sit in a circle. Have one child put his spoon in the middle and sing the song (to the tune of "The Farmer in the Dell") using the child's name. Continue until all spoon children are in the circle.

Discuss

Say, **King Josiah was only 8 when he became king. He did what he knew was right. How easy is it for you to act responsible? You know you shouldn't litter. Do you? If you are responsible you don't. How else can you be responsible?**

My Bible Teaches Me Responsibility

29

That's What the Bible Says

song

• • • • • • • • • • • • •

Directions

Sing to the tune of "The Hokey Pokey." Teach the class the hand motions first. Continue the song with the left hand, feet, head, whole body, etc.

I'll put my right hand up,

I'll put my right hand down.

I'll put my right hand up,

And I'll wave it all around.

I'll be responsible, and I'll only do what's right.

That's what the Bible says!

Responsible Like Joash

craft

. . . .

Materials
- king pieces, duplicated
- crayons or markers
- paper fasteners
- scissors

Directions
1. Have the class color and cut out the king pieces.
2. Show how to attach the parts to the body at the dots using paper fasteners.

Usage
This craft may be used as a memory verse incentive. Have Joash keep his arm down until the verse is said, then have him raise his arm in triumph when the verse is repeated.

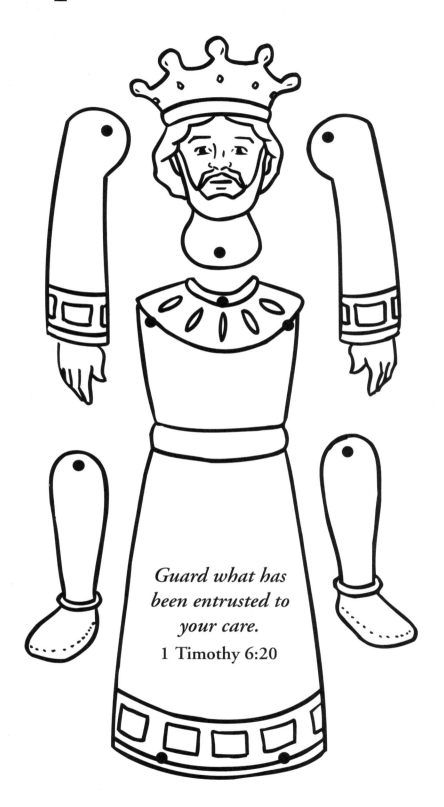

Guard what has been entrusted to your care.
1 Timothy 6:20

I Am Responsible When...

game

Materials

- strips, duplicated
- box with a hole large enough for a hand to fit through
- toothbrush
- washcloth
- Bible
- feather duster
- pencil
- paper
- dog bone

Directions

1. Have a child pick a strip, then, by feeling, find the corresponding object in the box (for example, "good health" is represented by the toothbrush).
2. Without talking, the child should act out how to be responsible, using the item and the statement on the strip as a theme. The rest of the class should guess what the child is "saying."

I am responsible for good hygiene.

I am responsible for daily devotions with God.

I am responsible to keep my room clean.

I am responsible to do my homework.

I am responsible to take care of my pets.

Responsibility Mobile

I WILL BE RESPONSIBLE

I promise to
_____

I promise to
_____

I promise to
_____

craft

Materials

- crowns and scroll, duplicated
- scissors
- rulers
- markers or crayons
- string or yarn
- hole punch

Directions

1. Have the students color and cut out the mobile parts.
2. On the crowns, they should write three ways that they will be responsible. They should write their names on the scroll.
3. Using rulers, have the children measure and cut three pieces of string — 6", 8" and 12" — and one length of string for hanging.
4. Allow them to make holes in the scroll and crowns at the dots using the hole punch.
5. Show how to tie the string to attach the crowns to the scroll and for hanging.

My Bible Teaches Me Responsibility

activity

Materials

•church and parts, duplicated
•scissors
•construction paper
•crayons
•glue

Directions

1. Say, **What happened to God's House? The doors and the windows are broken! Can you help to make the church look as though someone respects it?**
2. Have the class color and cut out the church and parts.
3. They should glue the church on the construction paper, then glue on the parts where they belong. They may glue on the verse strip wherever they desire on the page.
4. Have everyone draw a walkway up to the church, then pretend to walk up to the church using their fingers and saying the memory verse at the same time.

God's House

Guard what has been entrusted to your care. 1 Timothy 6:20

Child Kings

Guard what has been entrusted to your care. 1 Timothy 6:20

A Responsible King

. . . .

Materials
- frame, duplicated to heavy paper
- camera
- scissors
- crayons or markers
- tape

Directions
1. Take a photo of each child. Have each child wear a crown and hold a makeshift sceptre, if available.
2. Cut out the frames and their center sections.
3. Have the students color the frames.
4. Tape the photos to the backs of the frames.
5. Use the pictures as a bulletin board display or post them to your classroom wall or door.

Discuss
Ask, **What do think it would feel like to be king? Joash was just about your age when he became king of Judah.**

My Bible Teaches Me Responsibility

Chapter 4
My Bible Teaches Me Kindness

Memory Verse

I have loved you with an everlasting love; I have drawn you with loving-kindness. Jeremiah 31:3

Story to Share
Kindness for Mephibosheth

King Saul was dead. Not only King Saul but also his sons, Jonathan, Abinadab and Malchishua, who had been killed in a battle with the Philistines. King Saul was only wounded in the battle, but he was so afraid of what the Philistines would do with him if they found him that he killed himself.

Soon the news came to the house of Jonathan: "The king is dead! The princes were killed in battle!" This was terrible news to the household. What would become of them when King David took over? David and Jonathan, Saul's son, had been friends, but evil King Saul had treated David terribly. "Run," they were commanded. "Run for your lives!"

Mephibosheth, Jonathan's son, was only 5 years old when these orders were given. He didn't understand what was happening, but he could sense the terror everyone was feeling. Mephibosheth's nurse grabbed him up in her arms and ran for safety, but in the confusion she stumbled and dropped Mephibosheth. The fall crippled Mephibosheth.

One day David, who was now king, was thinking about his dear friend, Jonathan. They had once made a covenant with each other to show love and kindness to each other's families. "Is there anyone left from the family of Saul?" David asked. "I would like to show kindness to them because of Jonathan."

David was delighted when he was told about Mephibosheth, Jonathan's lame son. Quickly he sent for Mephibosheth, who was extremely frightened when he heard of the summons. "What could King David possibly want?" he wondered. "Does he wish to kill me?"

When Mephibosheth entered the presence of the king, he fell on his face and said, "Here is your servant." King David sensed Mephibosheth's fear. "Don't be afraid, Mephibosheth. I want you to eat at my table every day and be a part of my family. All the land that belonged to your grandfather, Saul, will now belong to you."

Mephibosheth knew he did not deserve these wonderful things that King David did for him, but he was thankful for King David's kindness. He enjoyed the privileges reserved for the king's own sons for the rest of his life.

— 2 Samuel 9:1-13

Questions for Discussion

1. Is it always easy to be kind?
2. Do you like it when others are kind to you?

craft

Materials
- hearts, duplicated
- red and pink paper
- scissors
- glue
- markers

Directions
1. Have the students cut out the hearts.
2. Show how to place the small heart pattern on the red paper and trace and cut out 14 hearts.
3. Similarly, they should trace and cut out 15 copies of the large heart on pink paper, then write one word of the memory verse on each.
4. Demonstrate how to alternate the big hearts and small ones, making sure the verse is in order, and glue together in a chain.
5. Tape the chains around the wall, close to the ceiling, for a "love"-ly border.

My Bible Teaches Me Kindness

Love Chain

I have loved you with an everlasting love;
I have drawn you with loving-kindness.
Jeremiah 31:3

Help Me Get to the King

Mephibosheth has been called to see King David.
Even though we know the King wants to be nice to him, our friend
Meph thinks the king wants to kill him!
Help Meph find his way to the palace to be blessed by King David.

puzzle

Materials
• puzzle, duplicated
• pencils

Usage
Even your youngest children can complete the maze since it does not involved reading. Have copies ready for early birds or to use as a filler at the end of your session.

*I have loved you with an everlasting love; I have drawn
you with loving-kindness.*
Jeremiah 31:3

Can I Be Kind?

Materials

- hand, duplicated to heavy paper
- yarn
- scissors
- pencils

Directions

1. Have the class cut out the hand.
2. They should write to whom they will be kind on the top line and how they will accomplish it on the bottom line.
3. Instruct the children to cut a piece of yarn, then tie it around the index finger on the hand as a reminder to be kind.

Discuss

Ask, **Are there people to whom you can show kindness? Is there someone in your neighborhood who is out of work? What about in your own home — could you do a chore that belongs to someone else?**

My Bible Teaches Me Kindness

I will be kind to

_____

this week by

_____

I have loved you with an everlasting love;
I have drawn you with loving-kindness.
Jeremiah 31:3

Hand-Clapping Kindness

Song

I love you,
Yes, I do.
With everlasting love,
I'll be true.
I love you,
Yes, I do.
With loving-kindness,
I'll be true.

song

. . . .

Directions

Sing to the tune of "Pease Porridge Hot." Teach the children how to do the clapping pattern at left as they sing the song. Allow them to make up new verses as you continue clapping.

Clapping pattern

Word 1: Clap your hands together.

Word 2: Clap your right hand with your partner's right hand.

Word 3: Clap your hands together.

Word 4: Clap your left hand with your partner's left hand.

Word 5: Clap your hands together.

Word 6: Clap your hands with your partner's hands.

Continue in this pattern until the end.

My Bible Teaches Me Kindness

Keeping Promises

craft

Materials
- badges, duplicated
- tape recorder
- cassette tape
- scissors
- tape

Directions
1. Have each child think of a kindness promise for the coming week.
2. Record them as they say their promises: "This is Timmy. I promise to make my sister's bed on Tuesday."
3. Stress that the promises need not be large, but they do need to be kept.
4. Cut out the Kindness Badges.
5. Play the tape the following week and ask who kept their promises.
6. Tape a badge to those who kept their promises.

KINDNESS PATROL

My name is _____

Jeremiah 31:3

Discuss
Say, **David** and **Jonathan** promised each other that they would show love and kindness to each other's families. Did David keep his promise? Yes! He showed kindness to Jonathan's son, Mephibosheth. Do you keep your promises when you make them? Have you ever promised your brother he could play with your ball, but when he asked again you said no? What about promising your mother you will help fold the laundry? Or help your father with a chore? Let's make some promises today and see if we can keep them this week.

Partner Fun

1. House of David, run to your partner and ask what he had for breakfast.
2. House of Jonathan, run to your partner and tell him your full name.
3. House of Jonathan, run to your partner and gently pat him on the head twice.
4. House of David, run to your partner and shake his hand.
5. House of Jonathan, run to your partner and say, "I love Jesus."
6. House of David, run to your partner and turn him around three times.
7. House of David, run to your partner and tell him your birth date.
8. House of David and House of Jonathan, run to your partners and say the memory verse.

game

. . . .

Directions

Have each child pick a partner. The partners stand opposite each other with six feet in between. One side is the House of David, while the other is the House of Jonathan. Call out the instructions at left for the groups to follow. Continue the game by creating and mixing up additional instructions.

Usage

This is an active game that can be as long or short as you desire. Afterwards, say, **You and your partner had fun playing this game together, just like Jonathan and David probably did** when they played together. David and Jonathan were good friends for a long time before David's kindness to Jonathan's son, Mephibosheth. David honored his friendship with Jonathan by being kind to his son. How can you show kindness to your friends' families?

My Bible Teaches Me Kindness

Mephibosheth

How many words can you make from the letters in Mephibosheth?

MEPHIBOSHETH

_____

_____

_____

_____

_____

Usage

Ask, **How many letters do you have in your name? Can you spell it? What if your first name was Mephibosheth!** Help the students begin the puzzle by suggesting a word, such as "cat." Allow them to self-score their work, then award a small prize for the one with the most points.

<u>Score</u>

2 points for each 2-letter word _____

4 points for each 3-letter word _____

6 points for each 4-letter word _____

10 points for more than 4 letters _____

Total _____

Partial list on p. 96.

My Bible Teaches Me Kindness

Kindness to All God's Creatures

craft

• • • • • • • • • •

Materials

For each feeder, you will need:
- 1 c. of peanut butter
- ¼ c. of cornmeal
- spoon
- bowl
- pinecone
- string
- plastic wrap

Directions

1. Have the students mix the peanut butter and corn meal in the bowl.
2. Show how to spoon it onto the pinecone.
3. Demonstrate how to loop the string through the top of the cone and tie to hang.
4. Say, **Hang your pinecone in a tree and show kindness to some hungry birds.**
5. Have everyone wrap their pinecones with plastic before leaving.

Chapter 5
My Bible Teaches Me Generosity

Memory Verse

A generous man will prosper; he who refreshes others will himself be refreshed. Proverbs 11:25

Story to Share
You Can Have It

Jesus was tired from teaching and healing. "I need to rest. Let's find a quiet place to pray," Jesus said to His disciples.

Taking a boat, Jesus and His disciples sailed to a deserted place across the Sea of Galilee. But the crowd who followed Jesus found where He was and crowded on the coasts to wait for Him to return. When they saw His boat returning they shouted with joy.

Jesus saw all the people, the ones who were sick or crippled and those who had questions to ask Him. Jesus' heart went out to the people who needed him. He spent the rest of the day healing the sick, and teaching.

Soon it was getting late and the disciples were getting worried. "Master, you need to send these people away to the farms and villages around here to find food," they told Jesus.

Looking at the thousands of people who had come to hear Him teach, Jesus said, "Is there somewhere we could buy food for them?"

"Buy food?" one of the disciples scoffed. "It would take six months of work to even buy bread for each one in this crowd."

"Is there anyone here who brought food with them?" asked Jesus.

The disciples searched among the crowd and found a boy who had brought his lunch with him. They brought the boy to Jesus. "I only have five loaves of bread and two small fish, but you can have it," the boy said to Jesus.

Jesus told everyone to sit down. He took the bread and fish and blessed them. Then He gave the food to the disciples and told them to feed the people. They were astonished to see that the young lad's small lunch not only fed all 5,000 people, but afterward 12 baskets were filled with food that was not eaten. By generously giving all he had to Jesus, the young boy not only had enough to eat, the crowd did also.

— based on John 6:1-13

Questions for Discussion

1. Do you have anything you could share?
2. Could you save money to put in the offering? Could you share time to help your parents?

puzzle

Materials
•puzzle, duplicated
•pencils
•stopwatch

Directions

Bring a stopwatch and alert the children at the two- and four-minute intervals. At each interval, have them add up the number of words they have found and write the number on the lines below the puzzle. Then allow them to finish. As they complete the puzzle, give them their total time to write on the last line.

Fishy Word Search

Can you find all of the words to the memory verse in the puzzle below? Some letters are used more than once. Look in all directions!

A generous man will prosper; he who refreshes others will himself be refreshed. Proverbs 11:25

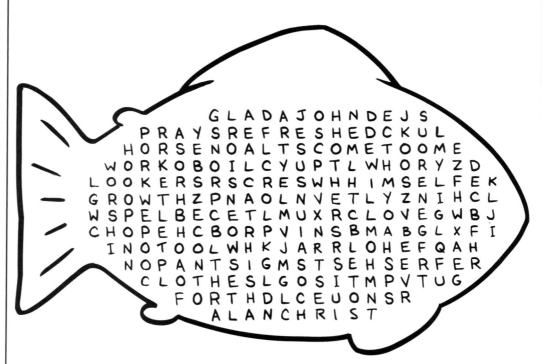

I found _____ words in two minutes.
I found _____ words in four minutes.
I found all of them in _____ minutes.

Solution is on page 96.

Sharing Multiplies Happiness

snack

Recipe to Share

2 slices of bread
1/4 cup of milk
2 drops of food coloring
unused paintbrush

Directions: Paint, toast and share!

A generous man will prosper; he who refreshes others will himself be refreshed.
Proverbs 11:25

Materials

For each child, you will need:
- two slices of bread
- ¼ cup of milk
- two drops of food coloring
- new paint brush
- bowl
- spoon
- plastic sandwich bag
- recipe, duplicated

Directions

1. Have the students mix the milk and food coloring.
2. Using a paint brush and the mixture, they may "paint" smiling faces or hearts on the bread (warn them to not make the bread too soggy).
3. Give the students bags to take their bread home, with a copy of the recipe at left. Encourage them to toast and share their treat with a friend. Or, bring a toaster to class and oversee the children as they toast the painted bread.

My Bible Teaches Me Generosity

Discuss

Say, **Sometimes when we are hungry it's hard to share; isn't it? Like when you have a piece of cake and your sister wants a bite, or a friend at school forgot his lunch and you only have one sandwich. What happened when the little boy shared his lunch with a multitude? Will that happen to your cake or sandwich? Sharing always multiplies your happiness!**

craft

Materials
- purse and coins, duplicated to heavy paper
- hole punch
- yarn, cut and ends taped
- scissors

Directions
1. Have the class cut out the purse and coins.
2. Show how to fold the purse backward on the dashed lines.
3. Help the students punch holes at the dots using the hole punch tool.
4. Give each child two lengths of yarn. Help them thread both lengths through the bottom middle hole and knot in back.
5. Show how to sew the yarn in and out of the holes in both directions. Bring both ends through the center hole and tie in front.
6. The children may race each other to put the coins in order. Then they may put the coins in the purse for keeping.

My Bible Teaches Me Generosity

Verse Purse

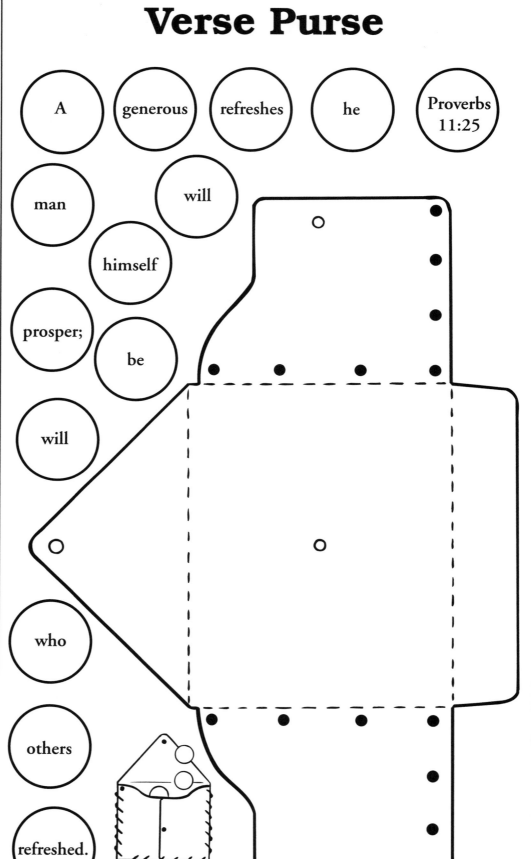

A generous refreshes he Proverbs 11:25

man will himself prosper; be will who others refreshed.

finished purse

When I Go to Church

O, when I go to God's house, to God's house, to God's house
  walking in place

Directions

Sing to the tune of "Did You Ever See A Lassie?" Teach the students the hand motions as illustrated first, then lead the song. Explain that being generous not only means giving money, but also giving our time and relinquishing our selfishness to be respectful and obedient.

O, when I go to God's house,
How generous I'll be.
    hands out in giving motion

I'll give to the offering,
    one hand cupped while other places "money" in

I'll help out my teachers.
    one hand out, then other hand

O, when I go to God's house,
    walking in place

How generous I'll be.
    finger to lips

My Bible Teaches Me Generosity

51

Time to Share

craft

• • • • • • • • • • •

Materials

- watch and hands, duplicated to heavy paper
- markers
- scissors
- paper fasteners
- tape

Directions

1. Have the class color and cut out the watch and hands. They should cut a slit in the end of the band at the rectangle.
2. Show how to attach the hands to the watch face with a paper fastener. Cover with tape to prevent scratching.
3. Help the students wrap the watch on their wrists, thread through the slit and tape to secure. You may need to cut some paper from the band to fit smaller arms.
4. Say, **Wear your watch to remind you it's always time to share.**

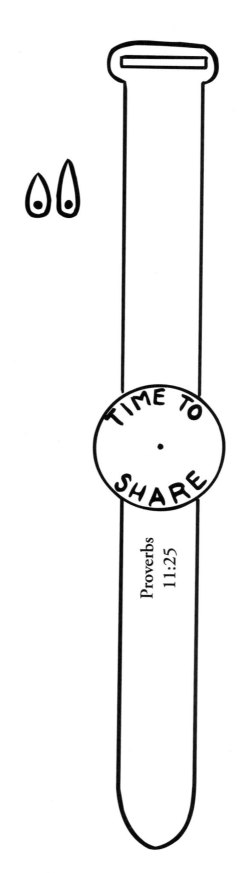

TIME TO SHARE

Proverbs 11:25

Sharing

3" x 3" pattern for 26 letters

craft

pattern for envelope label

SHARING IS FUN!

Materials
- plain square, duplicated 26 times
- label (at left)
- envelope
- marker
- glue or stapler

Directions
1. Glue or staple the label to an envelope.
2. Write a letter (A-Z) on each of the 26 squares and mix them up.
3. Hold up the squares and ask who can tell what they could share that begins with that letter. Give that letter square to the student with the first correct answer.
4. The one with the most letters at the end wins.

Variation
Add point values to the backs of the cards and total them at the end of the game.

Discuss
Say, **Do you have things that are so special you like to be the only one to touch them or play with them? Maybe you have a cowboy hat you just can't bear for anyone else to touch, or a doll that you don't want anyone else to hold** (let the students respond with the thing that is hardest for them to share). **What if the little boy would have felt that way about his lunch? Everyone would have gone away hungry. Instead, he received a special joy as he watched 5,000 others enjoy what he shared. You can experience that same feeling when you share what is yours.**

Generous With Me

action rhyme

• • • • • • • • •

Usage

Your younger students will especially enjoy this action rhyme, and it is a great way for you to review the themes of the lesson in a fun, memorable group activity. Teach the hand movements first, then read the script. Go through it several times to give everyone a chance to learn it.

I will be generous with myself,
Giving cheerfully.
> *cross hands on chest*

I will give my lips
To sing songs of Jesus' love.
> *point to lips*

I will give my hands,
To help my friends in need.
> *hold out hands*

I will give my feet,
To take me to God's House.
> *walk in place*

I will give my ears,
To hear my Pastor preach.
> *cup hands behind ears*

I will give my eyes,
To see what I can do.
> *point to eyes*

To be generous of myself,
Giving cheerfully!
> *jump, hands above head, legs spread*

My Bible Teaches Me Generosity

Bread and Fish

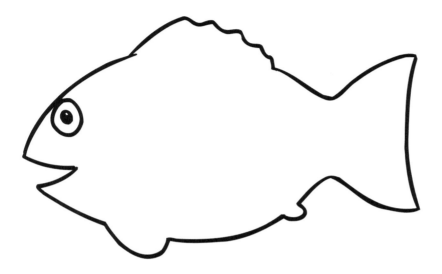

snack

. . . .

Materials
- small bread rolls
- cheese slices
- fish cookie cutter or plastic knife and duplicated fish pattern
- waxed paper

Directions
1. Give each child a piece of waxed paper, a roll and a cheese slice.
2. Pass the cookie cutter or the pattern and a plastic knife, allowing them to cut out their fish.
3. Encourage them to eat the scraps. Say, **Remember, Jesus didn't waste anything!**

Discuss
While they eat their snack, ask, **If your mother packed you a lunch, what would she put in it? Would you be willing to give that to Jesus?**

Variation
Take the children outside while you tell the story, weather permitting. Have the fish ready to eat right after the story.

My Bible Teaches Me Generosity

My Bible Teaches Me Obedience

Memory Verse

I am setting before you today a blessing…if you obey the commands of the Lord your God. Deuteronomy 11:26-27

Story to Share
Stinking Disobedience

"But I don't want to go to preach to Nineveh," Jonah argued to himself. "The Ninevites are wicked people and don't deserve God's forgiveness."

God wanted Jonah to go to Ninevah to warn the people to turn from their wicked ways or they would be destroyed. But Jonah hated the Ninevites and, instead of obeying God, went to Joppa and boarded a ship sailing to Tarshish. He immediately fell asleep, glad he had run away from God. But we can never run away from God and Jonah was about to find that out.

The ship had not been on the sea for long before a mighty storm blew up. It whipped water around the ship; the ship was tossed up and down and rocked back and forth. All of the men were fearful. They knew that the ship would soon break apart. Terrified, the sailors threw everything they could overboard.

The captain found Jonah sleeping. Shaking him awake, he yelled, "Wake up and pray to your God to save us!" But when the soldiers drew lots to find out who among them was causing the storm, the name drawn was Jonah's. "Throw me overboard," said Jonah. "I have disobeyed God and deserve to die."

As soon as Jonah was overboard, the sea once again became calm — no screaming wind, no swirling water. The boat again became easy to handle. But for Jonah, the terror was just beginning. God sent a giant fish to swallow Jonah.

Jonah was in the fish's belly for three days and nights. What a stinking place to be — and all because he did not obey God. He prayed day and night, thanking God for keeping him alive, begging God to forgive his disobedience and telling God he would obey Him if he had another chance.

On the third day, the fish spat Jonah onto dry land. This time when God told Jonah to go to Ninevah he did not hesitate. He was going to obey God!

— based on Jonah 1:1-4, 15; 2:1, 10; 3:1-3

Questions for Discussion

1. How easy is it for you to disobey someone who is in charge of you?
2. Do you think learning to obey your parents helps you to obey God?

craft

Materials
•strip, duplicated
•scissors

Directions

1. Have the class cut out the strip and snip at the slits.
2. Show how to curve the strip around so that the bottom slit meets the top slit (it will form the Christian fish symbol, as illustrated). Fit the slits into each other.
3. Instruct the students to throw the fish swimmer high into the air. They should try to say the memory verse before the spinner "swims" to the ground.

Fish Swimmer

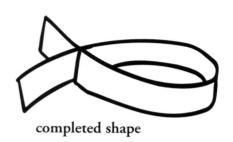

completed shape

I am setting before you today a blessing...if you obey the commands of the Lord your God. Deuteronomy 11:26-27

Where is Jonah?

Where is Jonah, where is Jonah?
tuck thumb under fingers

Here he is, here he is.
open fingers

Hiding in a big boat,
cover eyes

Running from our God.
Shame on him, shame on him.
make "shame" motions. shake head

Where is Jonah, where is Jonah?
tuck thumb under fingers

Here he is, here he is.
open fingers

Praying in a big fish,
fold hands in prayer

Asking for forgiveness.
He is sorry. He is sorry.
nod head

Where is Jonah, where is Jonah?
tuck thumb under fingers

Here he is, here he is.
open fingers

On his way to Ninevah,
"walk" fingers on arm

Going to obey God.
Good for him, good for him.
clap hands

song

. . . .

Directions

Sing to the tune of "Frere Jacques" ("Are You Sleeping?"). You may use this song to quiet down a boisterous class or as a break from individual puzzles and crafts. The class may remain seated as you teach them the motions, then sing the song several times through so they may learn it with the motions.

Coming Clean

activity

. . . .

Materials

- label (at right)
- empty, clean roll-on deodorant bottle
- liquid hand soap
- food coloring

Directions

1. Carefully pry off the ball of the bottle.
2. Fill the bottle with liquid soap, adding a few drops of food coloring.
3. Replace the lid and shake well. The soap will roll on.
4. Duplicate and glue on label.
5. Use this activity just before and after snack time to encourage clean hands. You may simply use the soap bottle, rather than the deodorant bottle, and glue the label onto it if desired.

My Bible Teaches Me Obedience

bottle label

SPECIAL CLEANING POTION

Discuss

Say, Let's pretend we are Jonah and the fish just spit us out! How do we smell? Can we get the fish smell do go away? Let's use this special potion to wash off the fish smell before we have our snack. Then we will thank God for helping us to obey Him like He taught Jonah.

Yummy Boats of Obedience

Materials

For each child, you will need:
- one hard-boiled egg, peeled
- 1 teaspoon of mayonnaise
- 1 teaspoon of mustard
- toothpicks
- sail pattern and recipe, duplicated
- scissors
- spoons
- bowls
- plastic knives

Directions

1. Show how to cut the egg in half and scoop out the yolk.
2. Have the children mix the yolk with the mayonnaise and mustard.
3. Show how to stuff the mixture into the egg halves.
4. Have the students cut out the sail and stick a toothpick through the slits. They may poke the sail in the "boat."
5. Distribute the recipe to take home.

My Bible Teaches Me Obedience

Recipe for Yummy Boats of Obedience

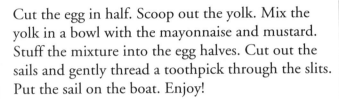

- one hard-boiled egg, peeled
- 1 teaspoon of mayonnaise
- 1 teaspoon of mustard
- toothpick
- sail pattern
- scissors

Cut the egg in half. Scoop out the yolk. Mix the yolk in a bowl with the mayonnaise and mustard. Stuff the mixture into the egg halves. Cut out the sails and gently thread a toothpick through the slits. Put the sail on the boat. Enjoy!

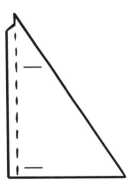 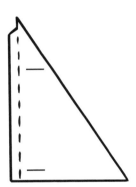

Sail Patterns

I am setting before you today a blessing...if you obey the commands of the Lord your God.
Deuteronomy 11:26-27

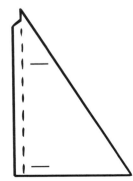 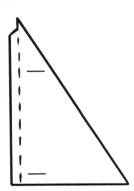

Materials
• letter, duplicated
• pencils

Directions

Help the students to consider what a fish might think to have a person in its stomach. What did the fish feel Jonah doing inside him? What did he feel as he spat Jonah onto the beach? What did he see as he was swimming away? Encourage creativity. Post the letters on your bulletin board or door when completed.

A Tale from a Fish

What do you think Jonah's fish thought when he swallowed Jonah?
He'd never had anyone praying in his stomach before!
Imagine what it must have been like for him.
Help him finish the page in his diary.

Dear Diary . . .

_____

_____

_____

_____

_____

_____

_____

_____

_____

_____

_____

_____

Jonah in Sequence

Materials
- story cards from pp. 63-64, duplicated
- crayons
- scissors

Directions
1. Have the class color and cut out the story cards.
2. Challenge them to put the cards in the order of the story.
3. Encourage the children to share their cards with friends and tell them the story.

Variation
Read the story on page 57 aloud again to your students. Ask them to hold up the story cards at the appropriate times.

My Bible Teaches Me Obedience

Nutty Obedience

My Bible Teaches
Me Obedience
*I am setting before
you today a blessing…
if you obey the commands
of the Lord your God.*
Deuteronomy 11:26-27

Finished Craft

craft

Materials
- fins, tail and verse, duplicated to heavy paper
- walnut shell halves, clean
- poster paint or markers
- clear nail polish
- glue
- scissors
- magnets
- wiggly eyes
- scissors
- smocks

Directions
1. Have the students paint the shells.
2. After the shells dry, they should coat them with polish.
3. Have them color and cut out the fins and tail.
4. Show how to glue them to the nut.
5. Allow them to glue on wiggly eyes.
6. Show how to glue the nut to the memory verse strip, leaving the verse at the top.
7. They may glue a magnet on back.
8. Say, **Take this fish home to remind you what happened when Jonah disobeyed God!**

My Bible Teaches Me Obedience

Chapter 7
My Bible Teaches Me Forgiveness

Memory Verse

Forgive whatever grievances you may have against one another.
Forgive as the Lord forgave you. Colossians 3:13

Story to Share
David Forgives Saul

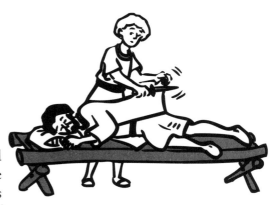

David and his army were hiding from King Saul. He slept and lived in a deep, dark cave, not daring to show his face because he knew that if the king found him he would be killed. While he was in the cave, King Saul and his men were hunting for David as if he were a wild animal.

"If only the king didn't hate me," David thought sadly. "I've done nothing but good for him. His son Jonathan is my best friend." David raised his head and looked toward the mouth of the cave. Startled, he stood up and looked more carefully. He could hear movement in the distance.

"Come here quick," David called to his men. "What is that I see? Is that the king and his men?" "Yes, and it looks like they're headed towards this very cave," replied one of David's soldiers.

Without any more thought, they hid themselves deep in the cave. Soon they heard voices. "It is so hot! I'm getting tired." That voice was King Saul's! David and his men did not make a sound. They could hear rustling and knew King Saul and his army were settling down to rest. Not until they heard their quiet breathing did one of them speak.

"David," whispered one of his men. "Now is your chance. Kill King Saul and you will be king." "No," said David shaking his head. "I cannot kill God's anointed king."

Crawling toward King Saul in the darkness, David made sure all were sleeping. Very quietly, he cut off a piece of King Saul's coat and crawled back out of sight.

When King Saul left the cave, David called to him. "My lord, the king!" he exclaimed. Startled, King Saul whirled around. David fell down before him and bowed his head. Holding up the cloth he had cut from the King's robe, he said, "Why do you believe I wish to harm you? See, I was so close to you I could have killed you and I did not."

When King Saul saw that David could have killed him, he wept. "You, David, are a better man than I am. God be with you and may you have a long reign as king of Israel."

— based on 1 Samuel 24:1-17

Questions for Discussion

1. Have you ever had to forgive someone who did something wrong to you?
2. Is there anything we can do for which God will not forgive us?

67

Forgiveness Game

Directions

1. Have the first child in the class say, "My sister lost my baseball and this is what I'll do: Forgive."
2. Then the next person says, "My sister lost my baseball and this is what I'll do: Forgive whatever."
3. Continue, having the children add a word of the memory verse until they have said the whole verse.
4. Older children may change what needs to be forgiven each time: "My brother ate the last piece of cake; Jacob pushed me down; Susie hit me; etc."
5. Make copies of the verse at right for the students in case they need to refer to it. Prompt those who need assistance.

Forgive whatever grievances you may have against one another. Forgive as the Lord forgave you. Colossians 3:13

David's Forgiveness Knife

place this edge along the folded side of the paper

craft

. . . .

Materials

- knife and pouch, duplicated
- aluminum foil
- glue
- scissors
- white paper

Directions

1. Duplicate the knife to heavy paper. Use copy paper for the pouch.
2. Have the class cut out the knife and pouch pattern.
3. Show how to gently wrap the blade in foil and glue.
4. Instruct the students to trace the pouch pattern onto the edge of a folded piece of paper, then have them cut it out, being careful not to cut the fold. Have them write the verse on it and color it.
4. Have the class glue the sides and bottom of the pouch.
5. Place the knife in the pouch.

My Bible Teaches Me Forgiveness

Forgiveness Exchange

Have half of the children ask each other, "Will you forgive?" The others should answer, "I will forgive as the Lord forgave me." Then have them change places.

teacher help

• • • • • • • • • • •

Materials

• 8½" x 11" paper
• scissors

Directions

1. As you tell the story of David (on p. 67), fold the paper in half lengthwise.
2. Starting at the bottom, about ¾" from the fold, cut a straight line (illustration at right shows entire cutting pattern).
3. About 3" from the top, make a 2" sideways cut, then angle up to the end of the paper, ending at the fold.
4. Open the "sword" and write FORGIVENESS on it.

Variation

Give the children a piece of paper and scissors and teach them how to make their own "swords." Then encourage them to go home and tell the story to a friend, using a new piece of paper.

My Bible Teaches Me Forgiveness

Telling the Story

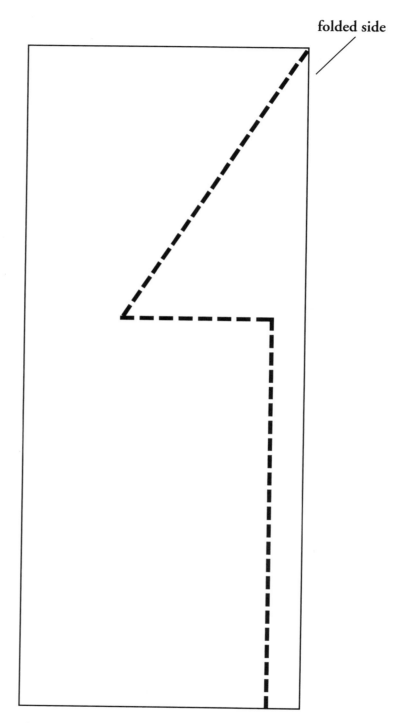

folded side

Approximate pattern of cutting (not to scale)

Scrambled Mess

David's men wanted to tell what happened in the cave,
but they got some of the words all mixed up.
Can you help straighten them out?

nikg   _____

vdida   _____

aevc   _____

usal   _____

bero   _____

Materials
•puzzle, duplicated
•pencils

Usage
After the students complete the top puzzle, ask them to tell what each word has to do with the Bible story. When they have finished the memory verse puzzle, have them practice memorizing the verse with a partner.

Bonus!

David forgave King Saul. What does our Bible tell us to do?

_____ whatever grievances you may have
grievfo

 against one another.

_____ as the Lord
ogfiver

_____ you.
fgovaer

— Colossians 3:13

**My Bible Teaches
Me Forgiveness**

Forgiving Makes Me Happy

craft

• • • • • • • • • •

Materials
• circles, duplicated
• pencils
• crayons
• scissors
• wiggly eyes
• yarn
• glue

Directions
1. Have the students cut out the face circles.
2. Allow them to glue wiggly eyes to the face and draw on a nose and other features.
3. Have everyone cut 1"-2" pieces of yarn for hair and glue it to the back of the face circle.
4. Show how to glue the front and back circles together, leaving a space open at the bottom for the eraser end of the pencil.
5. Pass out pencils so everyone may attach their happy faces on top. Sing the song together.

My Bible Teaches Me Forgiveness

Forgiving Makes Me Happy

God Forgave Me

Sing to the tune of "The Muffin Man."
(Allow alternate children to insert words in blanks.)

Do you know you should forgive, should forgive, should forgive,

Do you know you should forgive, like God forgave you?

Yes, I know I should forgive, should forgive, should forgive,

Yes, I know I should forgive, like God forgave me.

I will forgive my _____ , my _____ , my _____ .

I will forgive my _____ , like God forgave me.

David's Spear

David's Spear Recipe

Ingredients

toothpicks
raisins
fruit-flavored cereal circles
apples

Directions

1. Start with a raisin and thread it onto a toothpick, alternating with the cereal circles until you reach the end of the toothpick.
2. Cut apple wedges in V-shapes for the spearheads.
3. Pierce the toothpick handles into the apple spears.
4. Enjoy!

Forgive whatever grievances you may have against one another.
Forgive as the Lord forgave you.
Colossians 3:13

Materials

•toothpicks
•raisins
•fruit-flavored cereal circles
•apples
•recipe, duplicated

Directions

1. Start with a raisin and thread it onto a toothpick, alternating raisins and cereal circles.
2. Cut apple wedges into V-shapes for spearheads.
3. Pierce the toothpick handles into the apple spears.
4. Distribute recipes for students to take home.

My Bible Teaches Me Forgiveness

73

Army Puppets

craft

Materials

- puppets, duplicated from pp. 74 & 75
- glue
- scissors
- crayons
- hole punch

Directions

1. Have the students color and cut out the puppets on the outer solid lines.
2. Show how to fold them on the dashed lines and lightly glue together, avoiding glue at the bottom hole area.
3. Instruct the students to use the hole punch to make holes for their fingers at the dots on each puppet (each finger hole will require several clips from the hole punch).
4. Have the children use their puppets to act out the story as you read it.

Story

David and his men were hiding in a cave.

King Saul hated David and wanted him to die.

King Saul and his men came looking for David.

They looked and looked and looked — no David!

Then King Saul took a nap in David's cave.

"Hurry, come on," David's men said.

"Now's your chance to kill King Saul."

But all David did was cut a piece of the king's robe.

"I could have killed you, King Saul," said David.

King Saul cried and said, "God be with you."

King Saul

Soldier

David

Chapter 8
My Bible Teaches Me Honesty

Memory Verse

Do not lie to each other. Colossians 3:9

Story to Share
Untruthfulness Never Pays

After Jesus went back to heaven, the disciples were faithful to Him. There were about 5,000 people who worshipped at Jerusalem. Some of the believers had plenty of money for their needs, others had only enough for food and necessities. And there were those who didn't even have enough for food.

"Peter, I've been thinking about some of the people in our congregation. There are those who need money for food and clothing," said Barnabas. "So I've sold a piece of land. Take the money I received from the sale and use it to help these people."

Other people who had plenty did the same. God blessed the congregation. There was not one among them who was hungry or did not have clothes or a place to live.

Ananias and his wife, Sapphira, had a piece of land, too. "Do you think we should sell our land to give to the poor?" asked Sapphira. "I've been thinking about it. The others are doing it, maybe we should too," answered Ananias. So Ananias and Sapphira sold their land. But when they saw all the money…

"Oh, Ananias, look at all this money. Do we have to give it all to the poor?" asked Sapphira. "Why don't we give most of it, but we'll pretend we gave it all," schemed Ananias.

When Ananias presented his gift to Peter, Peter said, "Ananias, you have given in to the temptation of Satan. This land was yours to do with as you wished. You did not have to give it to the needy. You have lied to God." When Ananias heard these words, he fell down and died.

Sapphira, wondering what happened to her husband, came to Peter. Peter asked her, "Is this the amount of money you and Ananias sold your land for?" "Yes," lied Sapphira. "We wish to help the needy." Peter was astonished. "Sapphira! How could you and Ananias agree to lie to God? Your husband is dead and you will die also." And Sapphira, too, fell down and died.

The people of the church were very afraid when they realized how much honesty means to God.

— based on Acts 5:1-11

Questions for Discussion

1. Is it easy for you to lie? How do you feel after you lie?
2. Will God forgive you for lying?

puzzle

Materials
•puzzle, duplicated
•pencils

Usage

Review the memory verse with the class before distributing this puzzle. Provide Bibles so they may look up the verse in Colossians after they complete the puzzle.

Memory Verse Mail

Making a continous line, can you spell out the memory verse in the block below?

Do you have an address?
Of course you do!
Your memory verse has an address, too.
It's Colossians 3:9.
Now that you know what the verse's address is, you can go see it.

Solution is on page 96.

Honesty Pantomime

Narrator: The early church was a happy, growing church. But there were some people who were needy. And others had plenty. The ones who had plenty helped those who were in need. Some even sold land and brought the money to the church.

Peter: *kneels in prayer*

Barnabas: *brings bag of money and gives to Peter*

Peter: *takes money, pats Barnabas on the back and shakes his hand*

Ananias & Sapphira: *takes money out to look at it; shakes head and puts all but a few coins back in bag*

Ananias: *takes money to Peter*

Peter: *takes bag; holds out hands as if saying, "Is that all?"*

Ananias: *nods head*

Peter: *shakes finger at Ananias*

Ananias: *falls as if dead*

Peter: *covers Ananias with a blanket*

Sapphira: *enters, looking around*

Peter: *shows bag; holds hands out again*

Sapphira: *nods head*

Peter: *shakes finger*

Sapphira: *falls down as if dead*

Narrator: Ananias and Sapphira lied about how much money they received from the sale of their land. God was not happy. He punished them for their dishonesty. Colossians 3:9 says, "Do not lie to each other." I'm going to try to be honest, how about you?

Directions

Select children to the be Peter, Barnabas, Ananias and Sapphira. You may want to serve as the narrator. You will also need two small money sacks (any type of filled sack will work) and a blanket. Either provide copies of the pantomime to each actor or call out the instructions. If desired, do the skit several times so every child can play a role.

My Bible Teaches Me Honesty

Materials
- puzzle, duplicated
- pencils

Usage

Most students will be familiar with true/false worksheets, but they may need assistance with remembering details of the Bible story. For younger children, you may want to read through each statement and have the class answer as a group.

True or False

Read the sentences below. Does the underlined word make the sentence true or false? Write "true" if the sentence is true. If the sentence is false, write the word that would make it true.

1. Before Jesus went back to Heaven, He told His <u>sisters</u> to go and preach the gospel.

   _____

2. There were about <u>thirty</u> people in the church at Jerusalem.

   _____

3. Barnabas sold his <u>car</u> to give money to help those who were in need.

   _____

4. <u>Ananias</u> and his wife, Sapphira, had a piece of land to sell.

   _____

5. They didn't want to give all the money to the <u>bank</u>.

   _____

6. Ananias and Sapphira lied and said they gave <u>all</u> the money they received from the land.

   _____

7. Ananias and Sapphira both <u>were happy.</u>

   _____

8. God says, "Do not <u>lie</u> to each other."

   _____

Helpful Story Tellers

craft

. . . .

Materials
- story pictures on pp. 81-82, duplicated on heavy paper
- scissors
- markers or crayons
- magnets
- glue
- tape player
- cassette tape
- metal surface

Directions
1. Make a tape of yourself reading the Bible story on p. 77.
2. Have the class color and cut out the story pictures.
3. Show how to glue magnets to the backs of the pictures.
4. Play the tape and allow the children to place the pictures on the metal surface at the correct time.

Variation
Use felt or Velcro on the backs of the pictures for students to attach them to a felt board.

My Bible Teaches Me Honesty

81

Singin' About the Bible

1. *The More I Read My Bible*

O, the more I read my Bible, my Bible, my Bible,
O, the more I read my Bible,
The happier I'll be.
"Don't lie to each other," it plainly does say.
O, the more I read my Bible,
The happier I'll be.

Directions

Sing #1 to the tune of "Did You Ever See A Lassie?"

Sing #2 to the tune of "This Little Light of Mine." For fun, have the boys stand and shout, "Don't you lie" and have the girls stand and say, "Only tell the truth."

Sing #3 to the tune of "Jingle Bells."

2. *My Little Bible Says*

Don't you lie, not once (oh no!)
Only tell the truth.
Don't you lie, not once (oh no!)
Only tell the truth,
Tell the truth, tell the truth, tell the truth.

3. *Careful What You Say!*

Please don't lie,
Please don't lie,
Careful what you say.
Honesty is always best,
'Cause lying never pays.
Ohhhhh.... (sing again)

My Bible Teaches Me Honesty

83

puzzle

....

Materials
•puzzle, duplicated
•pencils

Usage
Have this puzzle ready for early arrivers or as a time filler. Even new readers will be able to recognize the letter shapes that are different from "X" and write them on the line. Go over the answers with the class when everyone has finished.

My Bible Teaches Me Honesty

Too Many Lies?

Someone told too many lies and now we can't find out what our Bible is teaching us today. Cross out all of the X's and see if you can find the hidden word. Write it on the line below.

XXXHXXOXXXXNXXXEXXSXXXXTXXXXYXXX

_____

Now, see if you can find our memory verse in all of the Xs, then write it on the lines. Do you have it memorized yet?

XXXDXXXXOXXNXXXOXXXXTXXLXXXIXXXXETXXXXX
XXOEAXXXCXXXXHXXOXXXXXTXXXHXXEXXRXXX
XXX.XXXCXXXOXXXLXXOXXXXXXXSX
XSXXXXXIXXAXNXXXXSXXXXXX3XXX:XX9XXX

_____

_____

_____

Solution is on page 96.

84

My Bag of Coins Reminder

craft

Remember Ananias and Sapphira:
Honesty Is Best!
Acts 5:1-11

Finished Craft

Materials
- tag, duplicated
- 8" circle of brown suede
- small rocks
- twine
- hole punch

Directions
1. Have the students select several rocks. You may either have these ready or take the class outside to find their own.
2. Show how to place the rocks on the middle of the suede, pull it around the rocks and tie with twine.
3. Allow the students to use the hole punch to make a hole in the tag at the dot. Then they should thread one end of the tied twine through the tag and knot.
4. Encourage the children to put the bag where it can remind them of the Bible story and to tell the truth.

My Bible Teaches Me Honesty

Chapter 9
Miscellaneous Bible Activities

DEAR PARENT,

We are studying about the Bible, that wonderful Book God has given to us.

We would like for your child to bring a Bible to class each week.

If your child does not have a Bible, we would be glad to provide one. Please contact me at:_____

THANK YOU!

_____

Supply Help

Directions

Duplicate and distribute the note. Check off the items you need and insert the date on the blank line when you want them brought in. You may issue one note at the beginning of the eight lessons or issue one note per week or every few weeks, depending on your needs.

Dear Friend,

We are learning about the wonderful book God has given to us — the Bible.

There are a few items we could use to complete the activities in our lessons. I have checked off those that we need on _____.

❑ aluminum foil
❑ apples
❑ bread rolls
❑ bread slices
❑ cereal circles, fruit-flavored
❑ cheese slices
❑ clothespins
❑ cornmeal
❑ craft sticks
❑ deodorant bottles, roll-on
❑ eggs, hard-boiled
❑ envelopes, letter-size
❑ food coloring
❑ gelatin, Knox and flavored
❑ grocery bags, paper
❑ handsoap, liquid
❑ magnet bits
❑ mayonnaise
❑ mustard
❑ nail polish, clear

❑ paint brushes, new
❑ paper fasteners
❑ peanut butter
❑ photo of your child, small
❑ pinecones
❑ straws, plastic drinking
❑ plastic wrap
❑ raisins
❑ sandwich bags
❑ self-stick plastic, clear
❑ spoons, plastic
❑ stickers, church themes
❑ straws, plastic drinking
❑ string
❑ suede, 8" brown scraps
❑ toothpicks
❑ waxed paper
❑ walnut shell halves
❑ wiggly eyes
❑ yarn

Thank you for your help!

_____
teacher

Miscellaneous Bible Activites

Bible Tree

God Gave Me My Bible

_____

My Bible Teaches Me Respect

_____

My Bible Teaches Me Responsibility

_____

My Bible Teaches Me Kindness

_____

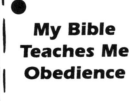

My Bible Teaches Me Generosity

_____

My Bible Teaches Me Obedience

_____

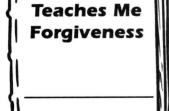

My Bible Teaches Me Forgiveness

_____

My Bible Teaches Me Honesty

_____

teacher help

. . . .

Materials
- Bibles, duplicated
- tree limb, 24" long
- bucket
- plaster of paris
- yarn
- scissors

Directions
1. Follow the package directions to fill the bucket with 6" of plaster of paris.
2. Allow the plaster to harden slightly, then stand the tree limb in it.
3. Give a sheet of Bibles to each student. Have them write their names on the lines and cut them out.
5. Provide a hole punch to make holes at the dots.
6. Show how to thread a piece of yarn through the Bibles and tie for hanging.

Usage
As you complete each lesson, tie a Bible on the tree for each child present. You may also have the children make their own trees to take home using a hairspray lid for the stand and a small branch.

Miscellaneous Bible Activities

Bible Charades

game

Materials
- character cards
- scissors

Directions
1. Cut out the squares and turn them upside down.
2. Have each child pick a square. Say, **Don't let anyone see who you have!**
3. Have the children act out a part of the story involving the character on their cards.
4. Whoever guesses the character correctly takes the square. See who has the most squares at the end of the game.

Variation
Have the child read the sentence on the card instead of acting out the character, then allow guessing as before.

Jeremiah
God sent me to prophecy against the city of Judah.

Baruch
I wrote down the words God gave to Jeremiah.

Elisha
Some young men laughed at me and called me a "baldhead."

Jesus
I became angry when I saw disrespect to the temple.

Joash
I became king when I was 8 years old.

King David
I was kind to Jonathan's son Mephibosheth.

Little Boy
I gave my lunch to Jesus and He fed 5,000 people.

Jonah
I disobeyed God and was swallowed by a big fish.

Saul
David could have killed me, but instead he forgave me.

Ananias
I died for my dishonesty.

"My Bible Teaches Me" Review

game

• • • • • • • • • • • • •

Directions

1. Duplicate eight Bibles using the pattern.
2. Write or type the scripture from each lesson on them.
3. Pass them out and have each child stand and read the scripture. The first child to stand and say, "My Bible teaches me _____," takes the Bible. The one with the most Bibles wins.

Variations

Write only the reference on them. Or, copy the Bibles to colored paper. Assign point values to each color. Play the entire review before you disclose the point values.

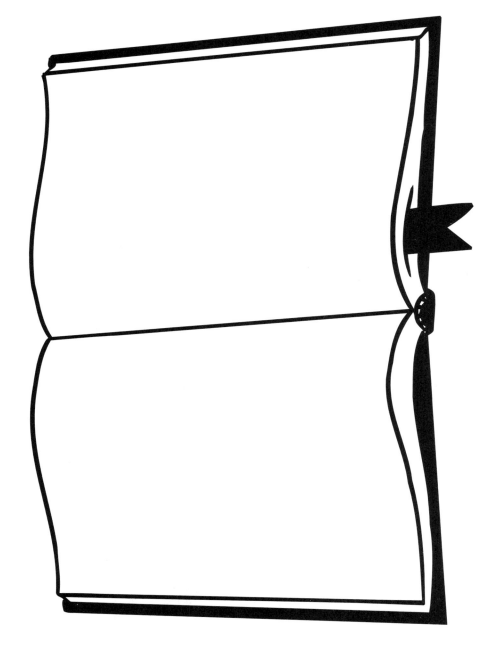

craft

• • • • • • • • • • • •

Materials

• Bible and rectangle, duplicated to white construction paper
• glue
• marker
• scissors

Directions

1. This craft works best if you enlarge the patterns on the copier machine.
2. Have the class cut out the Bible and the rectangle.
3. Instruct the students to write their names on the line on the rectangle.
4. With glue, have them trace over "My Bible Is My Teacher" and their name.
5. Show how to apply glue on the dashed line and attach the rectangle to the back of the Bible on the right side.
6. After the glue dries, tell the class to hold their Bibles up to the light to see an important message.

Miscellaneous Bible Activities

Secret Message

My Bible Is My Teacher

_____

Important Message!
Hold Bible up to light
to read your message.

Wiggle Busters for Little Bible Readers

My Bible doesn't do me a lick of good,
shake head vigorously

When its closed up as tight as a clam.
hunch shoulders, feet together, head to chest

No-sir-ree!
shake head vigorously

But it will do me a bundle of good,
nod head vigorously

When it's open for me to read.
open arms and spread legs

Yes-sir-ree!
nod head vigorously

Open,
open arms and spread legs

Close,
hunch shoulders, feet together, head to chest

Open,
open arms and spread legs

Close.
hunch shoulders, feet together, head to chest

I'll open my Bible each day.
spread arms and jump feet apart

Usage

Your younger class members will especially enjoy this activity. Teach them the motions first, then read the lines and do the motions together. Begin speeding up the words as they learn the motions and see who can continue correctly at faster speeds.

Miscellaneous Bible Activities

craft

Materials
- bookmarks, dupli-cated
- crayons or markers
- hole punch
- yarn
- clear, self-stick plas-tic
- scissors

Directions
1. Have the class co-lor and cut out the bookmarks.
2. Help the children to lay the book-marks on the sticky plastic.
3. Have them cut the bookmarks from the plastic.
4. Show how to punch a hole in the top of the bookmark.
5. Allow the students to string a few strands of yarn through the hole.

Optional
Duplicate several cop-ies for each child to make bookmarks for gifts.

Miscellaneous Bible Activities

Bible Bookmarks

Commemorative Stamps

. . . .

Materials
•stamp, duplicated
•construction paper
•scissors
•crayons or markers

Directions
1. Have the class cut out the stamp.
2. Ask the students to select a Bible character they studied to draw on the stamp. Remind them that the stamp can include the person's face and items related to his or her life. Help the students understand the concept (bring in a few commemorative stamps).
3. Cut large hearts from construction paper, glue the stamps on them and display them on a bulletin board with the slogan at left.

THE BIBLE IS STAMPED ON OUR HEARTS.

Miscellaneous Bible Activities

Answers to Puzzles

Fading and Enduring, page 11
Words find: rose, pansy, iris, peony, grass, tulip, mum, daisy, violet.
Leftover letters spell BIBLE.

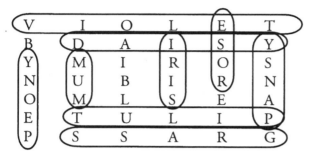

Respectful Rhyming, page 20
Show, per, to, one, Love, the, brother, be, Peter

Rebus Story, page 23
first blank: boy or girl
second blank: church
third blank: praying hands
fourth blank: preacher
fifth blank: Jesus

Crown Confusion, page 28
Guard what has been entrusted to your care.
— 1 Timothy 6:20

Help Me Get to the King, page 39

Mephibosheth, page 44
met, mob, pose, pot, hit, him, best, sob, hip, pit, she, this, them, bet, his, hop, hot, mop, Tom, Tim, the, poem, stop, step, pet, those, hose, hoe, shop

Fishy Word Search, page 48

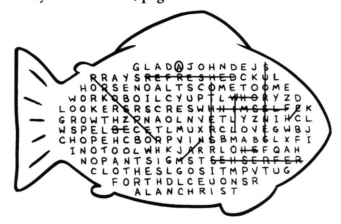

Scrambled Mess, page 71
king, David, cave, Saul, robe
Forgive, forgive, forgave

Memory Verse Puzzle, page 78

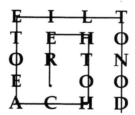

True or False, page 80
1. false, disciples
2. false, 5,000
3. false, land
4. true
5. false, church
6. true
7. false, died
8. true

Too Many Lies? page 84
honesty
Do not lie to each other. Colossians 3:9